HOW TO SELL YOUR HOME FAST AND FOR TOP DOLLAR

Mark Floyd

Prominence Publishing

Copyright © 2016 by Mark Floyd

Real Estate License: #0542155
All Rights Reserved.

Printed in the United States of America. No part of this book may be used or reproduced in any manner whatsoever without written permission except in the case of brief quotations embodied in critical articles or reviews.

Book and Cover design by Prominence Publishing. www.prominencepublishing.com

Note: A REALTOR® is a real estate professional who is a member of the National Association of REALTORS® and subscribes to its strict Code of Ethics. We understand that the use of the word REALTOR® cannot be substituted with "real estate agent," "real estate salesperson," or "property manager." Just because a person is a real estate agent, does not automatically mean they are a REALTOR®.

For more information, contact Mark Floyd at:
www.DFWHomePricing.com
www.DFWSold30.com

For a Free, No Obligation Home Evaluation to determine your home's value call:
(469) 371-5670

ISBN: 978-1536985740

First Edition: August 2016

CONTENTS

INTRODUCTION 1
   Dedicated to Serving Veterans 3
KNOW YOUR COMPETITION 5
   What Home Sellers Need to Know About Their Competition 5
   Features Matter 6
   How Your Realtor® Can Guide You 7
UNDERSTANDING THE CURRENT MARKET 9
   What Are Homes in Your Market Area Selling For? 10
   The Market Can Change Overnight 11
   Winter vs. Summer 12
PRICING STRATEGIES 13
   How Pricing Affects How Quickly the House Sells 13
   How a House Can Sell Quickly and Still Get the Most Amount of Money 14
   About Bidding Wars 16
PREPARING YOUR HOME FOR SALE 19
   How to Prepare Your Home for Sale 20
   Preparing a Tenanted Home for Sale 21
STAGING TO SELL 23
   The Benefits of Staging 24
   Staging Success 25
INSPECTION PITFALLS 27
   When Things Go Wrong 27
   Recommended Inspections for the North Dallas Area ... 28

- When the Inspection Indicates a New Roof is Required 30
- How to Prepare For the Inspection 31

LIVING IN YOUR HOME WHILE IT'S FOR SALE . 33
- Why It's Important to Have the House Ready to Show at All Times 33
- How to Make It Easier to Keep Your House Ready to Sell at All Times 34

NEGOTIATING YOUR BEST DEAL 37
- Negotiating with Buyers and Buyer's Agents 38
- The Benefits of Using a Realtor® 40

MARKETING (DO'S AND DON'TS) 45
- Marketing to Sell Quickly and For Top Dollar 46
- Unique Marketing Customized to Your Needs Makes a Difference 50
- The Problem with Holding Open Houses 51
- Holding an Open House for Real Estate Brokers 52

OTHER TIPS AND STRATEGIES FOR HOME SELLERS 55
- Tip: Before you accept an offer, call the lender to learn more about their situation 57
- Tip: You must have good communication! 57
- Tip: Choose the right Realtor®; pick someone who will work for your best interest 58

CONCLUSION 63
ABOUT THE AUTHOR 65
WHAT PEOPLE ARE SAYING ABOUT MARK 67
RESULTS 69

INTRODUCTION

"First comes thought; then organization of that thought, into ideas and plans; then transformation of those plans into reality. The beginning, as you will observe, is in your imagination."

~ Napoleon Hill

When I was a kid in elementary and middle school, I used to sneak candy into my backpack at school and sell it to my classmates. I think I've always had the sales bug. As I got older, I would find things that people wanted and make those things available to them. I grew up in the Dallas, TX area and saw how quickly things were changing in the north Dallas housing market just after 2005 and that really got me interested in real estate. When I started out, much of my neighborhood was just empty fields and farmland. Then when the real estate market started heating up, you'd see whole neighborhoods go up what seemed to me to be overnight.

All these homes were being built and that fascinated me because our community was changing so quickly. I had graduated from high school in the north Dallas area and joined the Air Force in 1997 because I was young and adventurous. I like to travel and I enjoyed meeting and experiencing different cultures. From there, I was stationed in Florida and then in the United Kingdom. When my enlistment was coming to an end after about 6 years, I decided to move back to the Dallas area to go to college. I got accepted to the University of North Texas.

At first, I thought I would major in Business, but one of my classes was real estate. At the time, it was hard for me to stay awake in the classes because they were so big and the professors went on and on about business. I learned quickly that I wasn't as interested in business as I was in real estate. My real estate classes really kept me engaged and that was the first time I was really interested in a career field. I majored in Marketing and Real Estate and I got my degree from University of North Texas in 3 years.

After graduation I did what most students do – I went looking for a job. I thought that my experience in the military and my new degree would help me land a career; however, it was not what most employers were looking for. I also had enough credits to get my real estate license so I took the test and passed it the first time. You would be surprised to learn how many agents fail the test their first or second time. And then a funny thing happened – people started to hire me to sell their homes.

My first client was somebody who was having trouble selling their home; their agent wouldn't return their calls, and they couldn't market the home effectively. They asked, "Mark, do you think you can sell our house?" I said, "Yes!"

Within about a week, I had interested buyers in that house and I sold it for exactly what they were looking for. That's when I discovered that I was really good at marketing homes. I know what buyers are looking for and I can provide good customer service. After that, I wasn't looking for a "job" anymore; I started my real estate career.

I like the challenge of marketing a property and working with sellers and buyers closely to accomplish their goals. You're selling for the most money in the least amount time. If it's a buyer, you are trying to find them the best deal and make everybody happy in the process.

Dedicated to Serving Veterans

Because of my military background, I really value getting the opportunity to work with veterans. In 2016, I helped a disabled combat veteran get into a home. At that time in the North Texas area, it was a buyer's market, so it was a challenge for anybody to get a home. I helped her get into a home in one of the hardest markets—in the North Dallas area. She was from the Northeast and got transferred here with a job. She always had a dream of owning a house and she was able to take advantage of special veterans financing with a VA loan. She was ecstatic. Now, she's a homeowner and building equity and living the American dream.

CHAPTER ONE

KNOW YOUR COMPETITION

"The ultimate victory in competition is derived from the inner satisfaction of knowing that you have done your best and that you have gotten the most out of what you had to give."

~ Howard Cosell

Know Your Competition. If you don't know what you are up against, you can't find leverage to make the best deal happen when it's time to sell your home fast and for top dollar.

What Home Sellers Need to Know About Their Competition

Whether your home is worth $10,000 or $100 million, every seller wants the same thing - to sell for the most money in the least amount of time. Your competition is made up of your neighbors and other home sales in your local area. Think about your neighbors for a moment: if they are selling their home, and you are selling yours - you are competing with them.

How you compete could be on the asking price, the condition of the home, the features and/or the location. Does your home or theirs back up to a busy street, water tower, electric towers, etc.? That could change your value negatively or positively. The type of updates or lack thereof that you or your neighbor have done to the house also make a big difference. Of course, the asking price and days on the market are another factor potential buyers will consider.

Features Matter

What are the features of your home? Your neighbors' homes? Think about features that are items that buyers are specifically looking for such as a pool, a certain number of bathrooms, an upgraded or open style kitchen, whether or not there is an outdoor kitchen. All of those upgrades can change the price of your home versus your neighbor's house right down the street.

Keep in mind, buyers are not just viewing your home, they are also looking at your neighborhood homes for sale. How does your home compare? Is your kitchen larger, or do you have more bathrooms? That can increase your value. Does your carpet need to be replaced, whereas your competition has beautiful wood floors? That can decrease the interest in your home and ultimately your selling price.

How Your Realtor® Can Guide You

Your Realtor® should explain what to do, and what not to do to sell your home for the most amount of money. This means providing a neighborhood sales report that shows the sales price of the homes in the area, and how much money they are getting when they actually sell. I provide all sellers with a detailed report that includes pictures of homes so they can compare their home to their neighborhood sales.

I recently sold a home that was in need of repairs, and the seller was concerned that he would not get the price that he wanted. This seller was not aware of recent neighborhood sales, and the value he found online was low and inaccurate. I provided him with a list of active sales in his neighborhood along with pictures. We listed his home AS-IS and received multiple offers, and accepted an offer above the asking price within 5 days.

In another instance, a frustrated seller called me to say that he had his home listed with another agent, but was unhappy with the results. He asked if I could sell his home above asking price in under 30 days. He hired me and I showed him who his neighborhood competition was, and how his home compared.

He took my advice and we listed his home and received an above the asking price offer in about 3 days. We listed it for about the same price he was asking before, and sold it above that price! He had no idea that buyers were choosing other homes in the neighborhood over his house until he let me take over his marketing.

CHAPTER TWO

UNDERSTANDING THE CURRENT MARKET

"Insanity: doing the same thing over and over again and expecting different results."

~ *Albert Einstein*

Understanding the current market is everything if you are selling your home. Is it a seller's market or a buyer's market? Real estate markets move in cycles and a seller's market can quickly become a buyer's market. If you are selling in a favorable market, then you hold all the cards in the transaction. I advise my sellers to hold a firm position on price and purchase terms. My listings usually receive multiple offers so I like to see favorable terms like low or no closing costs for my clients.

What Are Homes in Your Market Area Selling For?

Asking price and selling price are totally different. What are the average days on the market? Time is money, and if your home has ever been listed for weeks and months you know this all too well. Many agents will get you to list your home for an unrealistic number and then hope that you will reduce your price when it fails to sell fast.

You should know exactly what home sellers are asking for, how much they are selling for, and then how many days they are taking to sell. You also want to know what the difference is between those sales and your home. This would be determined by the home size, location, bedrooms, bathrooms, pool, updates, repairs, etc.

Understanding your current market also includes understanding closing cost trends. Fees like title policy, closing costs, HOA fees, home warranty, and surveys are negotiable. If you have multiple offers, then you rarely pay such fees. This will net you more money when your home ultimately sells. Option period or inspection period money should be as large as possible to reduce the chances of the buyer backing out for little cause. This is the money you receive from the buyer to inspect the home and back out for any reason. The option period days should be limited also. Don't allow a buyer to have a 10+ day period to put your home under contract and then decide to back out on day 12.

In all market conditions some home sellers will struggle with selling, and some home sellers will flourish. Thousands of homes fail to sell in your market every year – even in the best of seller's markets. If you want to sell your home fast and for top dollar you have to understand your local market. When homes in your area are selling for $150 per square foot, the chances of you getting $200 may be too aggressive. Or, perhaps it is correct if homes in your area are outdated and your home is upgraded throughout. Knowing your real estate market is vital when selling, and buyers are willing to overpay for certain homes.

The Market Can Change Overnight

If your local area has a low inventory of homes and many buyers, then you can take advantage of high offers in little time. Likewise, if your neighborhood is full of homes for sale, you may not get the price you were hoping for. As homeowners see home prices quickly increasing they may decide to sell their homes and cash out. There is an old saying: "Buy low and sell high."

When you start seeing more real estate signs in your neighborhood then you can probably expect a plateau on selling prices. It is a simple matter of supply vs. demand. Low supply + high demand = higher selling price and a seller's market. High supply of homes + lower demand of buyers = lower selling price and a buyer's market.

Winter vs. Summer

Many people believe it is better to sell in summer vs. selling in winter. Actually, I see higher selling prices in winter simply because there are fewer homes available. Buyers are still looking in winter and even around the holidays. Most agents take the winter off because of this erroneous belief.

I sell more homes where I represent both buyer and seller simply because I do not turn off my marketing or my phone during winter. Remember, many buyers are being relocated due to their jobs, and this frequently happens between November - February.

Another example is when sellers view their property tax statement around spring time. The shock of higher property tax assessments causes many home sellers to put their homes on the market. This influx of homes can give buyers a greater selection of homes, and cause a mini buyer's market.

CHAPTER THREE

PRICING STRATEGIES

"All men can see these tactics whereby I conquer, but what none can see is the strategy out of which victory is evolved."

~ Sun Tzu

Pricing is crucial when selling your home and underpricing or overpricing your home could cost you thousands of dollars. There is a reason why the things you want to buy are priced at $9.99 and not $10. If your home is worth $400,000, consider pricing it for $399,000.

How Pricing Affects How Quickly the House Sells

If your house is overpriced, you will miss out on a large percentage of buyers who are filtering their online searches by price. You may also get a lot of people looking at your home, but no offers, because there are many similar properties in your area with a lower price. Chances are, you'd probably have more activity – even with a higher price – if you have good marketing in place.

How a House Can Sell Quickly and Still Get the Most Amount of Money

Let me tell you a story as an example about a house I sold in the M streets which is a very popular neighborhood in Dallas. Prior to my involvement, the house had been on the market for over 100 days with TWO different agents. It was marketed poorly and priced way above market value. My clients were looking to relocate to a different area of Dallas for access to better schools. They were really motivated because they wanted to get their kids into a new school before the next school year started, but time was running out for them to achieve that goal.

A lot of agents will agree to list your house really high just to get the listing. In that type of situation, they're hoping that somebody will give a lower offer to the sellers and cause them to eventually reduce their price. That's what happened to these sellers. Their original agents did not give them any advice on market niche, what amount to price the home at, or even take appealing pictures of the interior of the house! It's a beautiful home, and should have sold very quickly in that neighborhood.

After my analysis, I realized that they had overpriced it by about $100,000. That's a big difference. People are smart. When shopping for a home in that price range of $600,000 to $800,000, people are not going to overpay if they don't see exceptional quality. So their house didn't sell.

They contacted me and I met with them. I gave them honest advice and educated them about what's going on in the local real estate market. It was unfortunate that their first attempts to sell failed, but luckily they contacted me. I gave them the correct advice as far as marketing their home, what pricing they should be at, and showed them the competition.

If buyers were looking at their house, they were also looking around the neighborhood at other homes that were also for sale—so that was the competition. In this case, their house is the only different house in that neighborhood. Some other homes in the neighborhood were built as far back as the early 1900s, while their house was built in the early 2000s. Most of the homes there had wood floors, while their home had concrete floors.

Those are the kind of things I look for—the details. Those details make a difference in pricing and what type of buyer to look for. I gave them advice. They took 90% of what I told them and we had their home listed within a week. I then began my marketing campaign. We had about 10 showings the first day which blew them away because they didn't have 10 showings in the first several months previously listed with a different real estate broker. We had multiple offers and we were able to sell it above $720,000. We got them under contract within about two weeks. They were very happy.

They'd never sold a house before and the experience was interesting because they listed their house with other agents in the beginning. They were excited to be able to move forward with their plans and they got what they wanted out of the house. Setting the price properly at market value and using effective marketing strategies made all the difference to these sellers.

About Bidding Wars

Bidding wars are very common in most areas in North Dallas if your home is priced anywhere from $200,000 to $400,000. A "bidding war" is basically a multiple offer situation where you're looking for the best offer and you're sitting above asking price with little to no out of pocket costs paid by the seller.

To create competition, there's a couple of things an experienced Realtor® will do, First, you have to put your marketing in place to attract as many buyers as possible and you have to price it at market value. If you price it above market value, you're going to lose out on a lot of buyers who are willing to pay more, but are shopping for a deal. You also don't want to price it too low. If you price it too low, you're probably going to lose out on some of the high rollers as well. So you want to price it at market value. It's very common to see bidding wars or multiple offers in North Dallas right now.

In my real estate business, I offer an unheard of guarantee. **Your home SOLD above market value within 30 days guaranteed, or I'll pay you up to $10,000!** Without giving too much away, I can offer that guarantee because I typically sell more homes above market than the average agent. This is a unique guarantee. I don't know any other agents in the area who would guarantee to sell your house above market value in 30 days or less or pay you up to $10,000. The reason why I can offer that is because we already have over a thousand buyers in our database that are looking for homes. I would think that most sellers would want to work with an agent who already has buyers!

Our buyer database is a key benefit for our clients, because in many cases we already have buyers lined up before their home goes on the market for sale. Many of my recent sales involved buyers who were not even working with a real estate agent, and were drawn to my marketing. Another benefit of this is that our listings sell 55% faster and for 3.28% more money on average.

We achieve these results because we use aggressive marketing tactics. We don't just put a house on the MLS and pray that it sells. We take our time to offer valuable advice on preparing and staging the home for the best effect. We suggest things to do and things not to do to sell your home for more money, such as taking professional photographs to make the listing stand out. We recommend professional photos because most people are looking at these homes online before they even drive over to the neighborhood. They're going to be looking at them on their computer at home and photo size, quality and lighting can all make the difference between them coming to look at the home or passing it by.

Horrible pictures – for example, from somebody's cell phone camera – can turn a lot of people away. Or, if it looks like a hoarder is living in the house, it turns people away. We won't list homes that we know we can't market correctly. We offer sellers everything that they need to stage their home, market their house and find qualified buyers. The reason most of our listings sell for 3.28% more on average is because of our commitment to service and attention to those details. On average, we get higher offers.

CHAPTER FOUR

PREPARING YOUR HOME FOR SALE

"Where we love is home - home that our feet may leave, but not our hearts."

~ Oliver Wendell Holmes, Sr.

Sellers need to prepare themselves and their family before they put their home on the market. It is important for the seller to consider if they are going to be moving out of the area or staying in the area. I ask those kinds of questions before listing a home, because if the house sells quickly, they want to be prepared for that. I don't them want to be homeless. If they sell quickly they can find themselves homeless or in a tiny apartment.

How to Prepare Your Home for Sale

I've seen a lot of sellers buy a home before they list the house. That way, they are sure to have a place to go. That is nice because then you can move a lot of stuff out of your house. You could keep some of the furniture in the house while you're selling to stage it. I always say, "Prepare yourselves for the move before you even put your house in the market." You may want to box up and remove most of your personal items in order to declutter the home. It's all about the little things; for example, take clothes that you're not going to be wearing for several months out of the master bedroom closet. It will make the room seem less cluttered and the available storage areas seem bigger.

I recommend doing a pre-listing home inspection before listing your home. That can save the seller thousands of dollars versus having a buyer do an inspection that turns up costly repairs that need to be made or the offer falling through due to unresolved maintenance issues.

On a $150,000 house, you'd probably don't have to do staging. Instead I give sellers advice on things we need to do to improve the chance of selling fast. For example, we might need to professionally clean it, or remove pictures from the wall or remove things that are inappropriate or too personal. Remove any kind of visual distractions. If someone is busy looking at your art or staring at your fish tank, they aren't looking at your home with an eye to making an offer!

I have several different service professionals that I can call on: painters, handy people and cleaning companies that I recommend to my clients that need help getting their home ready to sell. That way they can get more than one quote or more than one bid.

Preparing a Tenanted Home for Sale

It can be a challenge to sell a house with a tenant. Especially if the tenant is not cooperative. You want to market the house to its fullest potential and you also need to make it available to buyers to go in and see. Selling your home with a tenant is difficult, but not impossible.

If the tenant doesn't want to show it, or if the showing does not work with their schedule, it can make selling the house more complicated. You really have to work closely with the tenant or it can become a challenge. If the tenant decides they don't want to move out when you've accepted an offer on the house, then you could have uncooperative tenants in the home to get out in order to close the sale. It all depends on the lease. You don't want to be in a position where you have to hire an attorney to do all the legal aspects of removing a tenant—that can cost a lot of money. That's why you want to have a good relationship with your tenant and so you can avoid conflict. The best case scenario is always to have the tenant move out and then put the house up on the market. Sometimes an empty house is easier to show than a lived in home.

CHAPTER FIVE

STAGING TO SELL

"Have nothing in your house that you do not know to be useful, or believe to be beautiful."

~ *William Morris*

Staging done right can be very effective; it can make your home sell fast and for more money. What type of staging you do and how much staging you need depends on the home and the location of the home. If it's a 10,000 sq. ft. home that's vacant, it needs to be staged. That's really going to pay off—depending on how good the staging is. If it's a vacant 2000 sq. ft. home, it probably doesn't need any staging. But, most homes need some kind of staging—especially when they've been lived in. Don't worry, staging doesn't mean you need to buy furniture or rent furniture and bring it into your house.

Sometimes, it means you need to take things out of your home. I see houses all the time with way too much furniture in a room and it makes the room look smaller than it really is. Things like decluttering your rooms, or removing pieces of furniture that you can put in your garage or in your attic, can really pay off by making the room look bigger. This type of staging makes the photos stand out. In marketing, we need the best pictures and if you have a picture of a room with excessive furniture in it, it's going to look cluttered and it's going to turn off some buyers.

The Benefits of Staging

The benefits of staging are simple. Homes that are staged usually sell for more money. If you want more money in your pocket, staging can help you accomplish that. People like pretty things. Buyers want something that looks nice and that looks big. Sellers are looking to get the most money out of their house. Buyers are looking for the best deal. It's as simple as that.

If they feel like, *"This house is beautiful, it's staged perfectly!"* and think *"It's my dream house,"* they will want to pay more—especially in this market we're in right now. This type of thinking is more likely if they can visualize themselves living there. It can make it easier for the seller to sell the house fast and for top dollar. I have examples of where the sellers didn't pay anything for staging and they got over $15,000 above the asking price on their home.

I recently sold a house for a client in North Dallas. I gave him staging advice by walking through his house and giving him a whole list of things to do to stage his home to sell. It didn't cost him anything except for time and he did everything I told him. He took my advice on pricing and we sold it within the weekend for $16,000 over the asking price.

Sellers can stage their own house. I walk through the home with them, room by room, and tell them exactly what they should do to market the home better. When we are showing buyers homes we hear their feedback, "I don't like this; I don't like that…" Or, we see them staring at the wall or this painting for 10 minutes when they should have been walking to the room and looking around. We know what distracts buyers and what they like so we share that with our sellers so that they're better prepared.

Staging Success

I remember this one house with a cow rug in the middle of the living area hiding the beautiful wood floors. It was like there was a dead animal in the house. I suggested, "Let's pull that out for our pictures and take it away."

If they left it there, they certainly wouldn't have any vegetarians or vegans looking at that house! It doesn't matter where it is – even if it's in an area where people hunt. You don't want to walk into a house where a giant grizzly bear is standing there. I wouldn't even walk into the rest of the house. I would be just staring at the grizzly bear.

I've done a listing for a man who had been trying to sell his house for years and years. I don't think he understood that the hunting gear and taxidermy animals in his house were contributing to the problem. It's distracting. It's like walking into a natural museum. He's got a bear, a leopard, he's even got a whole deer. He asked me, "Why can't I sell my house?" I told him the honest truth – he needed to take all his dead animals out of the house. Don't even put them in the garage. Take them far away. It really makes a difference.

CHAPTER SIX

INSPECTION PITFALLS

"A problem clearly stated is a problem half solved."

~ *Dorothea Brande*

Sellers should schedule their own pre-inspection on their home before showing the house to potential buyers. This one simple step could save you from unexpected news, delays or even loss of a sale on the house if a buyer's inspector turns up unexpected items that need repair.

Be sure to do a pre-listing inspection to find out what's going on with the house before you offer it for sale. You don't want any surprises.

When Things Go Wrong

With an inspection, it is always possible that the inspector might find a major problem with the house.

What if they discover that the pipes are broken? If you don't prepare for those kind of things, you're going to have a hard time selling your house. Also, it has to be disclosed if there's anything wrong with the house.

Let's say you did a pre-inspection before you list your house and discovered that the foundation needs to be repaired. If you take care of those items before you list your house, you're going to avoid a lot of problems and you're going to save money and time. If it doesn't get disclosed until after you list it and you have a buyer and you're under contract, you may not find that out for several weeks.

If you have your house on the market and now the buyer is asking for you to make all these repairs or threatening to back out, you've got a decision to make. Chances are if that buyer backs out on you now, you'd still have to make the repairs and find another buyer. It causes a lot more issues than if you took care of it beforehand.

Recommended Inspections for the North Dallas Area

I recommend a general home inspection, a termite inspection and then for homes that were built in 1980 and older, I recommend having your sewer lines checked and a plumbing inspection to check for leaks.

A lot of the plumbing lines that are cast iron have been known to fail. If the seller has that issue with their home, that can kill your deal and cost you tens of thousands of dollars to repair. If you're not working with a real estate agent, you should. Make sure you get all the inspections that you need on your home prior to closing on it.

Safety items are the number one thing to be aware of – things that can affect your safety and the safety of others. That would include things like gas leaks, electrical wiring and structural issues.

These are all important things that you need to be aware as they can potentially prevent somebody from getting a loan for the house. If the foundation is bad, if the roof is bad or there are some issues with the plumbing, those can be disallowed by lenders. Most lenders won't lend on a home that needs foundation work or roof replacement. They might not lend with plumbing issues or even missing appliances. The little things can add up. If there are a lot of little items in the home that need to be repaired, those can quickly add up if the seller is not calling the shots.

I've had buyers come back and request a whole list with 20 items to repair. If the seller decides to do that, it's just a long list of things. The benefit of getting a pre-inspection is avoiding these situations in the first place, and potentially saving a seller thousands of dollars.

Whether you are present during the inspection is up to you. I always say it's a good idea to be there towards the end, but you don't have to be there. The inspectors that I use give very detailed reports with good pictures. If you're going to be there for the inspection, the best time to be there is toward the end of it because it does take several hours. Also, be sure to stay out of the inspector's way even if you want to be there. If you stay, the inspector can run you through the summary of what they found. They usually tell you right then if there are any major issues.

I don't want families getting into a home that's going to be an unexpected money pit and needs a lot of work. Sometimes the inspection comes back with just a few things needing minor repairs. That's probably a house you want to move forward on. But, if for some reason, every time it rains the house turns into an island with water all around it, that's not a situation I want to get a buyer involved in.

When the Inspection Indicates a New Roof is Required

In the case of doing a pre-listing inspection, if it needs a whole new roof, I would definitely recommend the sellers contact their insurance company and file a claim because if there's any hail damage, then they'll usually cover that. All they'd have to pay is their deductible, if they have a deductible. They get an $8,000 to $10,000 roof, and then just pay the deductible.

If they're under contract and the buyer discovers a new roof is required, whether they find it out at the beginning of the contract, or they may find it out closer to closing, regardless, the seller is going to have to take care of that. No lenders are going to lend on a house that needs a new roof.

So if the buyer backs out now, they've been on the contract for weeks and months, now the seller has to replace the roof, and they have to find a new buyer. The seller typically will have to replace that roof unless it's being sold as-is.

How to Prepare For the Inspection

I would make things accessible and have all utilities turned on. Don't have boxes blocking the attic; inspectors usually want to have the walls clear so they can look at all the walls. On the exterior, don't pile up wood or bricks next to the house. Make sure the inspector can gain access to all areas of the house, inside and outside.

CHAPTER SEVEN

LIVING IN YOUR HOME WHILE IT'S FOR SALE

"Cleaning is my favorite way to relax. I clear things out and get rid of the stuff I don't need. When the food pantry and the refrigerator are organized, I feel less stressed."

~ Jennifer Morrison

If you want to sell fast you need to keep your home ready to show at all times and make your home available to show even when it isn't perfect timing for you. Think of it as a good start on packing for your move early.

Why It's Important to Have the House Ready to Show at All Times

Most buyers have jobs and schedules that may not mesh with sellers. They may not get off work until six or seven so they have a short window when they can go look at homes. That's usually the time when people want to go home and relax. You never know when buyers are going to look at homes, so you have to be ready.

We have secure electronic lockboxes which holds the house key. We also use a showing service that schedules the showings, keeps track of everybody who has shown the house and will request feedback from those agents continuously. And then once they give feedback, it emails that feedback to me and to my clients.

My showing service handles all the showings, they verify if the person is an agent, they schedule the showings and they keep the logs of everybody who shows the property. They also schedule appraisals and inspections. It's a tremendous benefit for sellers. This way, we know who's been in the house, we know when they were in the house and we're getting feedback from their visits. It helps everybody, especially the sellers.

How to Make It Easier to Keep Your House Ready to Sell at All Times

I'd recommend to be prepared to move because I'm going to sell your house quickly. So, put a lot of your stuff in boxes before we market it. You don't want to have a lot of items lying around when the photographer comes. You want to make sure your house is magazine ready for these pictures and for showings. That just means your house is going to be one of the nicest listed in the area so you can successfully compete with all the other neighborhood houses for sale.

You're not going to want that remote control in the picture. You're not going to want that picture of your kids showing up in a photo of the living room on the Internet home listing. You don't want a picture of a trash can. You don't want a picture of the laundry basket. You don't want a picture of your hair dye in the bathroom. Things like that. I tell clients to hide most of the things that we normally would keep out.

I would recommend they put a lot of stuff that they don't need into boxes, in the attic, or in the garage. For the 30 days they're selling their house (or less), it's best to live a minimalist lifestyle.

That's really the best advice for people who are living in their house and selling it. It's very hard to keep your house perfectly clean. Especially with kids. I have two kids, and that's the hardest part of keeping our house clean. Our kids always want to build forts or drag all their toys into the TV room.

When we sold our last house, I put all our stuff in boxes and I actually let them do it. It's like a game. I said, " Let's put this stuff in the box. We'll tape it up and we're going to open it at our new house. Write your name on it!" and we just packed everything away. When it was time to show our house, there were no toys, there was no clutter, it was all in storage in the boxes.

I recently sold a house where the owner cancelled with another agent after over 50 days on the market. The home was being lived in and I gave them advice on staging ahead of the listing. They had a ton of furniture in the house. More furniture than probably should have fit in there.

It was a married couple, with three or four children that were college aged and who walked in and out of the house at random times. It was kind of a challenging situation to show it, but I gave them advice on where they could put all these items. They trusted me—they did everything I said, and they put their stuff away. I prepared them for showings and we sold it; we actually got an offer above the asking price before it even went on the market and under contract in 48 hours. It can be done. You just have to trust in the advice of an experienced Realtor®, put in effort, and expect the results.

CHAPTER EIGHT

NEGOTIATING YOUR BEST DEAL

"The capability of negotiating... is something that means you not only have to understand fully what you believe and what your national interests are but in order to be a really good negotiator, you have to try to figure out what the other person on the other side of the table has in mind."

~ Madeleine Albright

Leverage is the key to negotiating the best deal for my clients. Whether I'm working on behalf of a seller or a buyer, I have their best interests in mind and I'm looking for the best way to get them what they are looking for out of the deal.

Negotiating with Buyers and Buyer's Agents

When I negotiate a sale, I want to make sure my clients have leverage so they can get the best possible deal. The best possible deal for a seller is obviously to get the highest sales price but also to give the lowest closing costs on their end. The sellers should not be paying for things like the buyer's closing cost. They should really not be paying for a title policy. It depends, but those things are negotiable. If a seller has multiple offers then they should consider not paying typical closing costs like title policy, some title fees and home warranties. I try to get my clients the most amount of money and that means negotiating out of as many of those fees as possible. So that's what I go into with the negotiation trying to achieve.

Also I try to determine how motivated the buyer is. How much do they love this property? If this is the only property they're looking at and they love this property, then my client has leverage and we have a better chance of getting the best deal.

I try find out how motivated the buyers are in conversations. I usually will start with, "Tell me a little bit about your buyer Mr/Ms Agent..." When you ask somebody a question they usually tell you more than they want to. They say, "Oh, my buyers love the property, their kids want to go to the local school." Or, they share that they really want be in the school district.

That kind of response tells me they are serious and really want the home. I say something like, "Great! We'll take a look at your offer and we'll get back to you." Now that we know these buyers really want this house, the sellers have leverage. In this market, anybody who gives you a really good offer and you have leverage over them, they're going to have a difficult time getting that house or negotiating it for lower sale price.

I recently sold a house in North Dallas. Again, it was with a seller who cancelled with another agent and the seller hired me. I gave them the advice that I typically give any home seller. We had it listed and we had 20 showings over the weekend.

We received an offer for about $7000 over the asking price and which was accepted. During the option period the buyer came back wanting to renegotiate the terms of the sale including the price, and was threatening to back out. It may have been a situation where the buyer was trying to get the home under contract and then attempt to renegotiate the whole deal.

What I recommended doing was, first of all, staying firm on price. This house had been on the market for maybe a week or so and in that time homes prices in the neighborhood were quickly going up.

We just held firm. We had leverage. You're not going to find another house with this price and we already had other people interested in the home. So why should we reduce the price? It made no sense.

We came back and said we want to increase the price but we're not going to reduce the price. The buyer had the right to back out but he was still within his inspection period, and the option period. They could have backed out, but they realized that it wasn't going to be a smart move on their end. For example, if the buyer backed out they would wind up paying more for another house because neighborhood home prices were increasing fast. We closed on it. My clients sold it for more money than they were previously asking for with the other agent and in less time.

The Benefits of Using a Realtor®

It can be disastrous to negotiate without a real estate agent working on your behalf looking out for your best interests. With or without a real estate agent, things can go wrong under negotiations because of poor communication. If they're not answering their phone, or they're not responding to email, the deal can just fall apart.

Like with anything else in life, if you are not communicating to resolve issues you're going to have a breakdown. That's the number one thing: poor communication. If the buyer doesn't have an agent, they're not getting any advice or they're getting bad advice from friends and family trying to be helpful.

I have people call me up all the time who are not represented, saying their Uncle told them this or that... I say, "Oh, is your Uncle a real estate agent in Texas?" "No," they reply, "but he sold a property in Alaska once..." I don't want to tell people that they don't know what they're talking about. I get called up for my listings all the time by somebody who is not represented by an agent and they say, "I don't want an agent. I want to represent myself because I think I'll get a better deal."

I usually ask them why they think that. It could be a ton of reasons but it usually comes back to they think they're saving money. In fact, they could be losing a lot of money. People think they can sell their house on their own. Some people think that they can sell their house and save thousands of dollars off the real estate commission.

If a Realtor® is able to get you more than the asking price by bringing in more buyers than you could ever do on your own, you could be losing thousands of dollars— walking away with thousands of dollars left on the table—simply because you thought you were saving money on the agent's commission. There's always somebody that wants to do it for cheaper but you usually can get burned by the results. You get what you pay for. If you pay for bad service, you're going to get bad service and bad results.

I have several examples where sellers were thinking about or trying to sell their own home and I was able to get them more money than if they had done a FSBO (for sale by owner). One of my sellers got an offer for $15,000 above asking price. Had he attempted FSBO he may have saved a few thousand on fees, but probably would have not attracted the number of buyers and would have netted less money at closing.

When you're selling a house by owner, first of all, you've got to get your home ready. You need to get the marketing in place. You've got to draft and prepare real estate contracts, you've got to talk to all of these different buyers and agents that come at you, if you have any buyers. So you've got to find buyers. You've got to talk with them and get them everything that they need and be fair to them.

All these different people, they don't necessarily have your best interests in mind. If you hire an agent to represent you and they're a good agent, they're going to have your best interest in mind which is selling your home for the most amount of money and getting the results you want.

Once you get an offer, it's not over. You have to make sure that you are up-to-date with everything that's going on with the closing. That means you have to communicate with the other agent, and with the buyer regularly, with the lender, with the title company and resolve issues that come about. It's a time consuming process to sell your house and if you do it yourself, my hat's off to you.

CHAPTER NINE

MARKETING (DO'S AND DON'TS)

"The aim of marketing is to know and understand the customer so well the product or service fits him and sells itself."

~ *Peter Drucker*

Marketing makes the difference when you want to sell fast and for top dollar. Not all Realtors® or real estate brokerages use the same marketing strategies. A lot of agents don't offer any marketing beyond the sign in the yard and a listing on the MLS. In today's market, that isn't enough to help your house stand out from the crowd, get noticed and sell fast!

Marketing to Sell Quickly and For Top Dollar

I implement my buyer and seller marketing plan. It includes pre-inspection recommendations, giving staging advice, arranging for professional photos, just to name a few items. I market my homes specifically to buyers. I don't market to other real estate agents. I don't market to other sellers. I market your house to a buyer because that's who we want you to sell your house to – buyers. I'm marketing to buyers that are currently in my database. I have a list of over a thousand buyers that have raised their hand and said, "Hey, I'm looking for a house in your area."

We have innovative strategies like the use of high end professional photographers. Most sellers don't use professional photographers with the latest techniques to really make your house stand out among the others.

My professional photography team might choose a high definition, top line camera, a 360 degree video, or a flying camera like a drone, depending on the property. Our job is to make sure that your home stands out among the others. Just as in any other marketing initiative, we want to outperform the marketing of that product.

We always follow the same method, whether it's a $100,000 home or whether it's a $100,000,000 estate, we want to offer sellers the best marketing. We use 24 hour talking ads that we provide on all our advertising— that basically gives buyer 24/7 access to information about your house. That way they're informed about your home and we can get them pre-qualified before they even step inside your home.

This really helps sellers because, for one thing, the buyers don't have to talk to an agent. All they have to do is call this talking ad hotline and get the information they're looking for. We find that we get three times as many calls off those ads because the buyers appreciate that they don't have to talk to an agent. For most people, they don't want to talk to a sales person at all. We put that number on the For Sale sign as well as all of the print advertising concerning that property. It has tremendous benefit to the seller because we're able to track those calls and give them all the information that they need or answer any other questions about the seller's home.

Of course we take full advantage of social media and internet marketing when selling your home as well. There are different online and social media programs we employ online which are directed at buyers. If you're selling your house, it's all about buyers. If you can't market to buyers or if your agent doesn't have the means to reach buyers, then there may be a breakdown in your sale.

Staging and photographs are a major component in marketing. I see homes all the time that fail to sell because the sellers didn't have any staging advice. When the house is very cluttered, then of course the pictures are horrible. In those types of cases, buyers won't even come to your house because of the pictures and because of that lack of appeal. Your typical buyer wants something that is move in ready and if what they're seeing in the marketing already looks bad, that's their first impression. They won't even come to your house to look inside. Everybody knows that first impressions are key. It's even more important when you're selling your house and if you have bad marketing, that's their first impression.

Marketing really starts online because that's where people start their search. 90% of people start their search online. Afterall, only 1% of buyers buy at an open house. When I'm selling a home, I'm going after the 90%. I don't go after 1% of the buyers. When people start their search online, they filter the results in terms of what the price range is and what their desired neighborhood is, so they're very specific about what they want. If your house is one of 50 that comes up but there's no pictures or the pictures are taken with a cell phone, or there's no staging, there's no proper lighting, they'll just skip right over it, it won't even be given a second chance.

I was working with a buyer in a tough Dallas seller's market, and was able to take advantage of a home due to bad marketing. Homes in this neighborhood do not stay on the market for more than a couple of days, and usually sell for well above asking price. This home had been on the market for more than 30 days without an offer, and the pictures online were horrible. It was a total mess and looked like a hoarder had been living there. As a result, no one even looked at it.

My buyer said, "I want to go and look at this house. I know the pictures are bad, but I want to go look at it." We went to look at it, and I was shocked. We walked in the house and it was beautiful! It was so nice inside. The pictures made it look haunted, but once you walked inside the home it was clean and bright throughout.

I would describe it as immaculate. It was so clean and updated, with a beautiful kitchen and brand new counter tops, and I didn't know what was going on. Looking online, it was horrible; it seemed like a completely different house. My clients loved it so we made a low offer, and it was accepted.

We were able to get this house below asking price—which is a challenge and almost unheard of in a seller's market. It all comes down to bad marketing and it really worked in my client's favor. If the seller only had had different advice, this house could have sold for a lot more money in less time. They just left money on the table. We saw that and we were able to benefit from that. That's an example of how bad marketing, even if you're working with an agent, can lead to less than favorable results.

Unique Marketing Customized to Your Needs Makes a Difference

I remember one unique situation where I sold a home in the North Dallas suburb of Plano TX. This seller had listed with another agent but it failed to sell after several months on the market. She hired me and I listed the home. The home was the largest in the neighborhood and was priced for a record area selling price. This house was perfect for an executive with a large family, or someone who needed a home office.

There's been a lot of news recently because many companies are moving their headquarters to Plano, TX. For example, companies like Toyota. All these businesses relocating to Plano is one of the driving forces for real estate prices going up. I quickly realized I needed to market this property to a buyer who may be relocating from the California area because that's where all the influx of people are coming from—Silicon Valley.

Based on this assumption, I set up a social media campaign and I quickly had several people contact me about homes because they were relocating.

As a result, I sold that house to a family that was being relocated from California to this area. These buyers found the home through my online marketing, and put in an offer without even viewing the home in person. It was a successful sale that sold for a record neighborhood price.

The Problem with Holding Open Houses

Holding an open house is not always a good idea for a seller. Most agents will tell that you need to hold an open house or you should hold an open house. What usually happens is that less than 1% of buyers come from an open house. So it's not the best way to get a buyer into a house. Also, most people that come and see the open house are your neighbors who just want to look around your house. They're not buyers. They are just nosy.

Then you've got people who walk into your house who have no intention of buying any time soon, they're not pre-qualified for a loan, they're getting your floors dirty, and basically wasting your time. So, I don't recommend an open house. The only people that benefit from open houses, or who think they benefit, are agents because they think they'll meet a buyer. Holding an open house is not a good marketing strategy.

Holding an Open House for Real Estate Brokers

If you have brokers who are actively working with buyers who are interested in a house in your area, holding a broker open house can bring in a new set of buyers. You see a lot of broker open houses on TV and that usually doesn't sell a house. It's usually just for show, just another party.

If a seller wants to hold a broker open house, I will hold one, but if I do hold one, I'll look for agents who have recently sold in that neighborhood where they for sure have qualified buyers that they can bring with them. So if that's one of your marketing strategies, it should be a very, very small part. Like I said before, 1% or less buyers come from an open house while the majority of them are coming from online or sales people or agents they've already contacted.

The only time that I hold anything that is really close to an open house (I call it a buyer tour) is when I have several inquiries about a house from buyers who are already pre-qualified. I contact each buyer and say, "I'm holding the house for 15 minutes today for pre-qualified buyers." I have them all meet me there at the same time. Having four or more buyers there at the same time and only giving them 15 minutes to walk into the house creates an environment of competition.

There's something about when you're walking through a house and you're considering buying it and other people have the same intention as you. It makes you want it more. You don't want to let them win. You want to win.

CHAPTER TEN

OTHER TIPS AND STRATEGIES FOR HOME SELLERS

"To be successful in real estate, you must always and consistently put your clients' best interests first."

~ Anthony Hitt

My experience works to make you more money and to help you sell fast. For example, I just sold a house that was, once again, previously listed with somebody else and they canceled or it expired. We sold it within about seven days. The seller is a very busy single dad with two kids and he works all the time. I went above and beyond to assist him with many aspects of the sale of his home. I was acting like a concierge for selling his house.

He had a couple of things he needed to do to his house before we listed it, such as landscaping. I scheduled that for him. I also scheduled the house cleaning and the floor cleaning for him. He simply did not have time to do it.

I didn't want him to be stressed out during the whole process and worrying and thinking, "When is my house going to get cleaned or when this is going to happen?" I was happy to take some of that burden off him. It's not that hard to call people and schedule for them to be there at certain times. It was worth it. We sold his house in under a week, and I helped him find another home quickly and without hassle. Now he's a client for life.

I want to take care of my clients. I've taken clients out for dinner. I've donated money to charity on their behalf. I really enjoy the personal aspects of my "job". Not only do I get to help them with their goal of selling their home, I also get to show them the way of giving back to the community. I like to give back to local children's charities. When I help people and donate locally, I have noticed that it's about more than money. Sometimes it's about giving back to the community.

Tip: Before you accept an offer, call the lender to learn more about their situation

Before you accept an offer, call the lender and find and what situation the buyer is in because that deal can quickly go sour. The person may have given the wrong information or perhaps the lender didn't get all the documentation that they needed to get a good approval.

Sometimes I recommend buyers to my lender who collects everything up front so there's no last minute closing issues. This is somebody I have worked with for about 10 years who has never failed to close a home transaction. They collect everything up front and do their due diligence so there are no surprises when you're at the closing table.

They look for pay history, if they're putting a down payment, their credit score, tax returns, things like that. Many times there are things that can surprise. For example, if the buyer's getting a divorce, that may destroy the deal. If the buyer buys a brand new car in the middle of the process that can destroy the deal as well. You have only so many days to find another buyer.

Tip: You must have good communication!

It all comes back to communication. You have to communicate with their lender to make sure that this is a qualified buyer. That's important. It can cause delays. It can cause your home not to sell.

There is still a lot of work to do even after you're under contract. Myself or my transaction coordinator regularly call up the parties involved: the agent, the lender and the title company just so we can keep in communication and make sure we're on track until a home closes. If we're representing the seller, we're calling the buyer's lender to make sure they have everything they need. Sometimes the other buyer's agent may not be doing it. I've run into that a lot of times.

The lender may say, "No, we requested this information from the buyer two weeks ago and we still haven't got it." Now, I have to call the buyer's agent or whoever to let them know, "Hey, we have a problem here. The lender's not getting the information they want and we're supposed to close in a week. What's going on?" That actually happens a lot and that's why we've learned to make sure we've contacted not only our side of the transaction but also the other side too.

Tip: Choose the right Realtor®; pick someone who will work for your best interest

At the risk of sounding like I bragging, I really have saved the day many times in a real estate transaction.

Once, I was selling a house, and we had it under contract fast. We received an above asking price offer within a couple of days. The seller didn't do the pre-inspection. It turns out he had a leak in the sewer line. Normally that would kill any deal if a buyer found out there was a leak in the sewer line.

I think the quotes we had was anywhere from $30,000 to $50,000 to replace the plumbing. Normally, any buyer would back away. The buyer wanted to back away but he really wanted to live in this particular neighborhood. Just when the buyer was about to cancel, he decided that he would take the home if the seller would agree to reducing the price by $50,000. The buyer had a quote for $50,000 from a plumber to make the repairs. The seller also received a similar plumber repair estimate that were both pretty close in price. This sale was about to fall through.

I found a better plumber. Someone was highly regarded and well reviewed in the area. He gave them a quote for around $30,000. When we thought this whole deal was going to fall apart because the buyer wanted $50,000 off the asking price. We were able to negotiate a much better deal based on the plumber I referred so that my seller was happy with the terms. In the end my client got what he wanted, and the best possible outcome.

I would say keeping a deal together like that is complex. Most people would not buy a house with a faulty sewer line. 90% of people would walk away from that.

The seller was prepared to take what the buyer was offering. We were able to get him around $20,000 more. The deal went through. We closed. My client, the seller, was able to buy and move into the house that he was working on.

In another instance, I was working with buyers that had been looking for a long time in a specific neighborhood. It just so happened that I was showing them a house in the neighborhood they liked when I got a notification on my phone of a new house that had just been listed a couple of doors down.

We walked out of the house that I was showing that they didn't like. I could tell they were very frustrated because they were looking for a home and hadn't found what they we're looking for due to low inventory. They were concerned they wouldn't find a house. I told them about this notification and that there was a home a couple of doors down. I said, "It's just hit the market. Let's go look at it." They were hesitant. There were no pictures. I scheduled the showing and we were the first ones in the house. They literally saw it within a couple of minutes of it being listed.

These buyers went from being discouraged to excited within a few minutes. They said "Mark, we want this house." I said, "We need to act quickly. We need to act right now." I rushed back to my office, wrote a full price offer, submitted it and I tried to use some leverage. I always try use leverage for my clients by saying they need an answer immediately.

The sellers responded right away and accepted our offer! A couple of hours later, the sellers received an above asking price offer from different buyers. More offers came rolling in. Soon the sellers realized that they had accepted our offer way too soon and got far less than they could have received. My client was still able to get the offer while they were at the original asking price. If we hadn't have been that quick, they would have been paying a lot more than that. They would have gotten into a bidding war.

Their case was tricky because they wanted a house with four bedrooms or more. It was a little over 3000 sq. ft. They were a new family and they wanted to be in this specific area of town with these specific schools. It was a first home purchase for them in a very prestigious neighborhood in North Dallas. There were not many homes that were exactly what they were looking for at that time. Homes generally ranged anywhere from $500,000 to over a million. They got a tremendous deal on that house. In that price range, in that neighborhood, it's very competitive.

CONCLUSION

"You don't climb mountains without a team, you don't climb mountains without being fit, you don't climb mountains without being prepared and you don't climb mountains without balancing the risks and rewards. And you never climb a mountain on accident - it has to be intentional."

~ Mark Udall

My philosophy about real estate is simple. You have to have a clear understanding of what the client's goals are, and a very strategic marketing system. I work with my sellers to establish the right price to list your home for, to get your home ready to be sold, to find a buyer and to negotiate the best possible terms for the sale of your home. I assist my clients in overcoming any obstacles and challenges along the way so that you can move forward and realize new dreams in your life.

In this book I've shared my insights in a straightforward manner in order to answer as many of your questions as possible so that you can feel confident when buying or selling your home. If you have additional questions or would like to learn more about selling your home, call me directly at (469) 371-5670.

ABOUT THE AUTHOR

Mark Floyd is a Dallas TX Realtor® and a Plano resident since 1977. Mark is an expert Realtor® in the Dallas Fort Worth area home market, and is very well respected by his clients and fellow agents.

Mark proudly served in the U.S. Air Force from 1997 to 2002, attended The University of North Texas in 2005 and graduated with a B.B.A. in Real Estate.

Mark has a reputation for being able to sell homes quickly and for top dollar.

For more information, contact Mark Floyd at:

www.DFWHomePricing.com
www.DFWSold30.com

For a Free, No Obligation Home Evaluation to determine your home's value, call (469) 371-5670.

WHAT PEOPLE ARE SAYING ABOUT MARK

"Show class, have pride, and display character. If you do, winning takes care of itself."

~ Paul Bryant

"Mark helped me from the beginning, giving me great advice on what to do to get the most value in the sale. It went on the market on a Friday night and was under contract the following Monday. And it was sold for the highest price in the neighborhood to date! Mark always kept in good contact and everything went smooth, I will definitely use him again when I'm ready to buy another home!" ~ Collin Prachyl

"Mark listed our house and immediately got us multiple offers and sold the house. We highly recommend Mark if you want to sell your house." Brooke L.

"Mark was fantastic to work with and was very responsive to any questions or needs. I've worked with a lot of Realtors® in my profession and he was one of the easiest to work with. I would like recommend his services!!" ~The Sim's

"Mark's knowledge of the market, his honesty and integrity with his clients, and his professionalism is remarkable. He has always considered his client's thoughts and concerns as a priority and I truly admire that. I will always work with Mark if possible." ~Xavier Luiz

"We are seniors who have had years of experience with Realtors®. Mark Floyd's unique sales approach enhanced our listing and brought us a qualified buyer within weeks. He has invested time and expense in equipment for aerial photos which leave nothing to the imagination. Unbelievable! Also, he is an awesome family man." ~The Langner's

RESULTS

3584 Green Acres Ter, Farmers Branch: "Cancelled" with another agent after 60 days on the market. Mark listed the house and received an accepted offer above asking in 24 hours.

2216 Micarta Dr, Plano: "Cancelled" with another agent after almost 20 days on market. Mark listed the property and received an accepted offer above asking in 3 days.

6018 Buffalo Bnd, Plano: Mark listed this home and received an accepted offer $16,000 above asking in 4 days.

1528 Jabbet Dr, Plano: Mark listed this home and received accepted offer above asking in 5 days.

5218 Merrimac Ave, Dallas: "Expired" with another agent after over 100 days on the market. Mark listed this house and received an accepted offer in 16 days.

2728 Royal Troon Dr, Plano: "Cancelled" with another agent after over 90 days on the market. Mark listed the property and sold it for a record neighborhood selling price!

10520 Faulkner Pt, Irving: "Cancelled" with another agent after almost 80 days on the market. Mark listed the home and received an accepted offer in 7 days.

www.ingramcontent.com/pod-product-compliance
Lightning Source LLC
Chambersburg PA
CBHW021441170526
45164CB00001B/330